# 38 Ways to Entertain Your Parents on Summer Vacation

by Dette Hunter
art by Kitty Macaulay

Annick Press Ltd.
Toronto * New York * Vancouver

# Contents

## Parents Unplugged

## Good Morning, Gull Lake

## Fun and Games



## Rainforest Hike

## Fun Lunch Contest

## Trophies of the Trail

## Dad's Bad Attitude

## Lakeside Spa

## Salsa Surprise Supper

## Fun In A Flash

To Charles, Amy, Claire and Samantha, who put the WOW in my summer.
—D.H.

For Tiki the Wonder Baby, and her cousins Zoe and Iris.
—K.M.

Some of the activities in this book require the use of a microwave oven. Kids should always carry out these activities under supervision.

# Introduction

Did you ever read a story where everyone is doing all kinds of fun stuff and think, "Hey, my family would love to try that!" Here's a book that lets you join right in.

Imagine that you are reading this story on a hot summer day. You love the part where they shake up some shivery ice cream. You can do it too – the recipe is right there. When the characters go for a walk in the woods, you can see what tracks to look for on your hike. And when they invent their very own board game, you can find out exactly how they did it right on that page.

Simon and Lily find everything they need to entertain their parents, and themselves, around their summer cabin. They turn paper plates into a wacky water game and an ordinary supper into snake stew and chocolate moose. And if you think newspapers are just for reading, think again … about swords, sun hats, bowls and butterflies!

So, if you're on vacation and worried that your family will be frustrated without friends, TV, computers and all the other stuff that keeps them happy at home, help is on the way.

Start off reading the story and when you find something that sounds like fun, try it out. Get everyone involved. You'll discover that the best part of summer is when your family has fun together.

Dette Hunter

The coolest thing about this old cabin is that the walls are so thin I can hear the loons on the lake

and my mom and dad talking in the living room.

My big brother, Simon, and I have huge plans. We're going to build a fort tomorrow. We'll have a secret password, handshake and everything. He would never, ever, have a secret anything with me in a zillion, trillion years if his friends were around … but they're not!

Simon's snoring. My kitten, Yoyo, and I are wide awake, listening. Mom's voice slipped through the thin pine boards. "I'm worried it might be a long few days with no friends, no TV."

"Very long, indeed," said Dad, "especially if it rains."

I couldn't believe my ears. My mom and dad afraid of being bored! Aren't they the very parents who said, "No TV or computers at the lake for us. The only screens this family needs are the kind that keep out mosquitoes."

When the first bird chirped, I woke up Simon.

"Mom and Dad need help," I said. "All that about not wanting TV or anything was just brave talk. I overheard them last night and they are big-time worried about being bored."

Simon took me seriously. Simon takes everything seriously.

"Unplugging themselves too quickly from their busy lives can be very traumatic, Lily," pronounced Simon, "especially if our poor parents have forgotten how to have fun."

"Does that mean we'll have to entertain them the whole time?" I asked.

"We will until we can teach them how to get by on their own. How can we have a fort when our parents are in peril?!"

# Parents Unplugged

Simon and I burst into the bedroom.

"We're here to banish your forebodings of boredom," announced Simon. (Simon sure sounded like he was on a quest all right.)

"You're what?" said Dad, from under his pillow.

"We're going to show you how to have fun, and getting up early is the best way to start," I explained.

"We are too sleepy to argue, so I guess we're in your hands!" Mom and Dad said and struggled out of bed.

"We'll start with a square meal," said Simon, as he got out rectangles of bread.

Dad took a deep breath of the clean country air. "Let's get cracking!" he said.

Simon got to crack the eggs.

Dad fried the dipped bread.

"Now for the fun!" said Simon. "Tic-tac-toast comin' up."

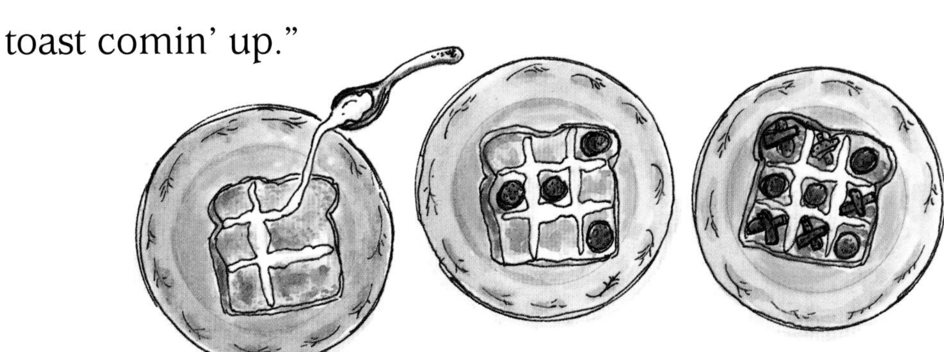

He drizzled strips of yogurt and made the lines. Then he sliced circles of sausage for the O's and used sliced strawberries for the X's.

## Tic-tac-toast

YOU'LL NEED:

- ☆ 2 eggs
- ☆ 1/2 cup (125 mL) milk
- ☆ 1/4 cup (50 mL) orange juice
- ☆ 1/4 tsp. (1 mL) salt

- ☆ 4 slices bread
- ☆ 1 tbsp. (15 mL) oil or butter

- ☆ yogurt
- ☆ sausage link
- ☆ strawberry

Crack the eggs into a bowl and beat well.

Add the milk, orange juice and salt. Beat until well blended.

Put oil into a frypan or griddle.

Dip one slice of bread into the egg mixture. Turn to coat the other side. Repeat with each slice.

Cook at med-high until the bottom is golden brown.

Turn over. Cook until the other side is golden. Remove from pan.

Place the toast on a plate and drizzle the yogurt in strips to divide the "board" into nine squares.

Slice the link of sausage in rounds for the O's.

Slice the strawberries into strips to make the X's.

Arrange on your tic-tac-toe board.

Serve with maple syrup.

## Peachy Pizza

YOU'LL NEED:
- 1/4 cup (50 mL) spreadable cream cheese
- 1 peach, peeled and sliced
- 2 tsp.(10 mL) brown sugar
- cinnamon to taste
- 1 English muffin, split in half

Spread cream cheese evenly over English muffin halves.

Arrange peach slices on top.

Sprinkle with brown sugar and cinnamon.

Broil until bubbly.

### Tip:

If you have the block-style cream cheese, thin with 1 tsp. (5 mL) sour cream or yogurt.

## Summer Kabobs

YOU'LL NEED:
- plastic drinking straws
- chunks of fresh fruit

Thread pieces of fresh fruit along the straw.

Use strawberries, blueberries, bananas, grapes, melon, kiwi . . . whatever you have.

Squeeze a lemon over the fruit to keep it fresh.

"Just coffee for me," yawned Mom.

A square meal is too edgy for Mom this early. But a nice, round peachy pizza will be just right.

Mom thought they'd taste even better if we browned them in the toaster oven.

I spread some cream cheese on English muffin halves.

Mom sliced peaches and we arranged them on top.

Then I helped her cut up some fruit. It looked sort of sad just sitting in a bowl. Not nearly as much fun as Simon's toast. So I strung strawberries, grapes and chunks of banana and apple on a straw.

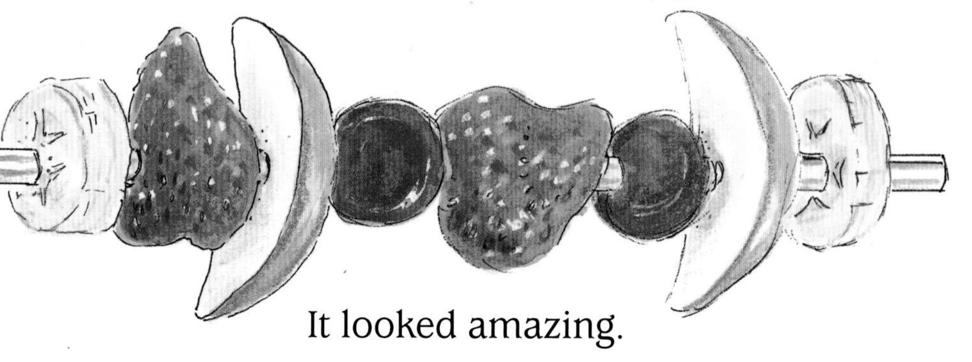

It looked amazing.

# Good Morning, Gull Lake

"Aggh … there's a bug in my mug!" said Mom, as she fished a ladybug out of her coffee.

"Ladybugs are not actually bugs," said Simon. "They are really beetles."

Mom frowned. Cities are Mom's thing. I could tell she missed the morning news and wasn't going to be ready to learn about bugs and stuff until she'd finished her coffee.

We emptied one of the boxes and made it into a TV.

## TV-in-a-box

YOU'LL NEED:

- ☆ sturdy cardboard box
- ☆ tape
- ☆ marker or crayon
- ☆ scissors or knife

Fold down the top of the box.

Seal with tape so it is closed on all sides.

Have an adult cut out a square from the front of the box and circles for puppet entry in the sides.

Draw knobs.

Dad cut a rectangle in the front and a place for hands on each side. I drew a few knobs and we had a TV.

## Quack Reporter Duck

Simon, Dad and I made a news team for our "Good Morning, Gull Lake" show.

YOU"LL NEED:

- ✯ paper (paper plate works fine)
- ✯ marker or crayon
- ✯ straw
- ✯ tape
- ✯ glue
- ✯ pencil

1. Trace your hand twice.
2. Cut out each hand tracing.
3. Tape the straw to one of the hands.
4. Glue together only at the palms.
5. Roll each finger around a pencil to make the 'feathers' curl.

My puppet reported about the mother duck and her fourteen fluffy babies who swam by this morning.

Mom smiled (maybe 'cause she only has two kids to keep track of in the water).

"You need a kitten on your news team, too," she said.

In a few folds Mom made a kitten that looked just like Yoyo.

"Purr-fect," I said.

YOU'LL NEED:

- ☆ square of paper
- ☆ crayon or marker
- ☆ drinking straw
- ☆ tape

1. Fold the square into a triangle with the fold along the top.
2. Fold in half to find the center. Unfold.
3. Use the fold to locate the center. Start the ears by folding the outer corners inward.
4. Finish the ears by folding upward as shown.
5. Turn over and draw face and whiskers.
6. Tape the straw on the back.

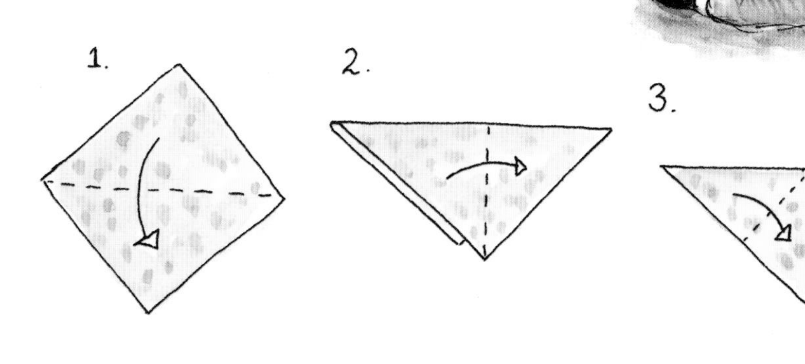

## Weatherperson Puppet

YOU'LL NEED:
- 2 paper plates
- stapler or glue
- crayons or markers

Cut a section (about 1/3) off one of the plates to make a space to slip your hand.

Draw your weatherperson's face on the other plate.

Staple or glue plates together.

"I'm Cumulo R. Nimbus, your morning meteorologist," said Simon, "and I have lots of weather on my plate today.

"I'm going to dish up a large serving of rain and clouds seasoned with occasional sunshine."

Simon cut a space for his hand on a paper plate and drew a face on another.

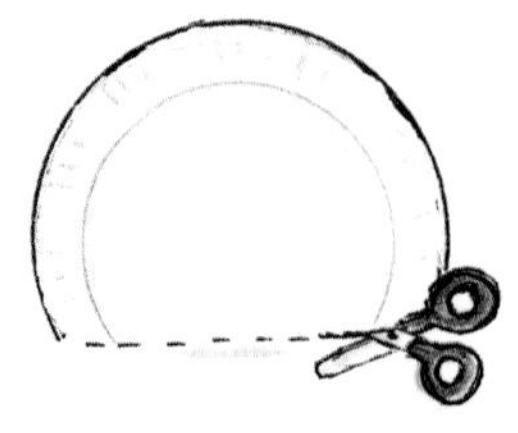

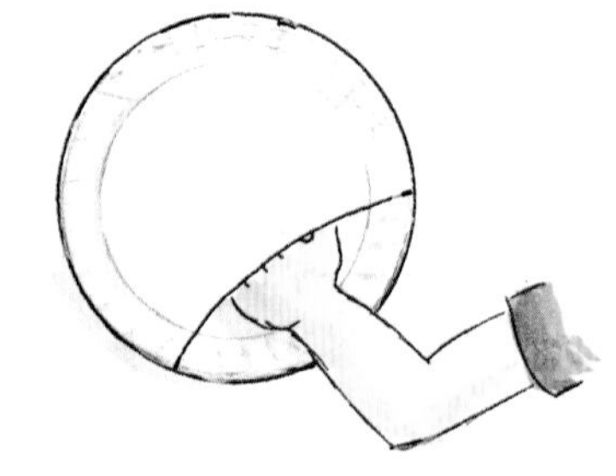

Dad drew a boat with a funny-looking thing hanging from it and held it in front of his face.

"I'm the anchor man," he said. I could see Dad had a long way to go as an artist, but he was trying.

Simon's weather report was right. It rained. We brought a billion boxes from home except the one with board games.

So we made our own sort of board, with coins for the checkers and our own rules.

## Never-be-bored Game

YOU'LL NEED:

- ☆ paper
- ☆ 4 pennies
- ☆ 4 nickels

Divide a piece of paper into 16 squares with a ruler and pencil or by folding the paper in half four times.

Arrange the pennies and nickels as shown.

One player moves pennies and the other nickels.

Take turns moving one coin in any direction but only one square at a time. No "jumping" over coins or sharing a square allowed!

The winner is the first one who gets all four coins in a straight line. The line can go up and down, from side to side or diagonally but must be on squares that are next to one another.

**Tip:**
As long as you can find a piece of paper and some coins, you'll never be bored during a long wait!

We kids won the first round of the tournament, but the parents were still in the finals.

"These aren't the rules we played by when I was a boy," said Dad.

"It seems you only complain about the rules when you're losing," teased Mom.

## Pinecone Pursuit

YOU"LL NEED:
- game board (paper plate, crayon or marker)
- counter (piece of paper, pencil, coin)
- a playing piece for each player (e.g. bottle cap, button, coin)
- pinecones

How to make:
GAME BOARD
With a crayon or marker draw your cabin in the center of a paper plate.

From the cabin mark off pathways that will lead to your favorite places.

While we waited for Mom and Dad to finish, we made up a game Simon called Pinecone Pursuit, 'cause every time we got to the place we were supposed to be we won a pinecone.

We made a special board and drew our favorite places on it.

We even made our own counter to see how many spaces to move.

Simon and I were having so much fun, we probably left Mom and Dad on their own too long. Their nattering interrupted our game.

"We wouldn't be having this discussion," said Dad,"if we hadn't forgotten the box of games."

"We wouldn't have," muttered Mom, "if you hadn't been in such a rush."

"That's it," said Simon. "Rain or not, we have to get them out of the cabin."

COUNTER

Divide a piece of paper into 6 sections and number them 1 to 6.

Put the paper on the table. In turn, each player tosses a coin on the paper to find out how many spaces to move. If it lands on a line, throw again.

**Tip:**

If you are on a beach you can make a counter like this by drawing the lines in the sand and tossing a shell or pebble.

| 1 | 2 | 3 |
|---|---|---|
| 4 | 5 | 6 |

HOW TO PLAY:

Each player chooses a small object to move around the board.

Then she chooses a place to visit and, in turn, throws the coin on the counter to see how many squares to move. She moves her piece that number of spaces. For example, Lily decides to hike to the beaver pond. She tosses the coin on the numbered paper and it lands on 3. She moves her bottle cap three spaces on the path to the pond. Now it's Simon's turn.

The player who gets to her chosen place and back wins a pinecone. Then she chooses another place to visit.

The player with the most pinecones wins the game.

## Rainforest Munch

YOU'LL NEED:
☆ a sealable plastic sandwich bag for each person

Toss together whatever assorted snacks you have hanging around your cupboard.

Here are some ideas: popcorn, raisins, dried apples or apricots (easy for kids to cut with small scissors), dry cereal (squares or rounds), sunflower seeds, pretzels, chow mein noodles, chocolate chips, small fish-shaped crackers, mini-marshmallows, banana chips.

Fill each bag (about 1 cup (250mL) per person) and seal.

"They won't be able to resist a rainforest hike," I said.

"Lily," said Simon, "this little woods is not really a rainforest. A rainforest is a special ecosystem made up of … "

"If it's got lots of trees," I interrupted, "and there's wet stuff dripping from them … I can call it a rainforest."

We knew Dad wouldn't last without a snack or two.

We cut dried apples and added them to the cereal, pretzels, and other stuff in a large bowl. We mixed it all together and put it in little bags.

We loaded it all in our backpacks.

I find forests a little scary, so I made up a song to scare away the bears.

We never saw even one bear.

## Lily's Song

Make a song for your family.

YOU'LL NEED:

☆ An easy tune everyone knows, like "Row, Row, Row Your Boat" or "Happy Birthday".

Make up your own words and be sure they rhyme at the end of each line.

## Trail Lessons (tracks)

## Trail Lessons (scat)

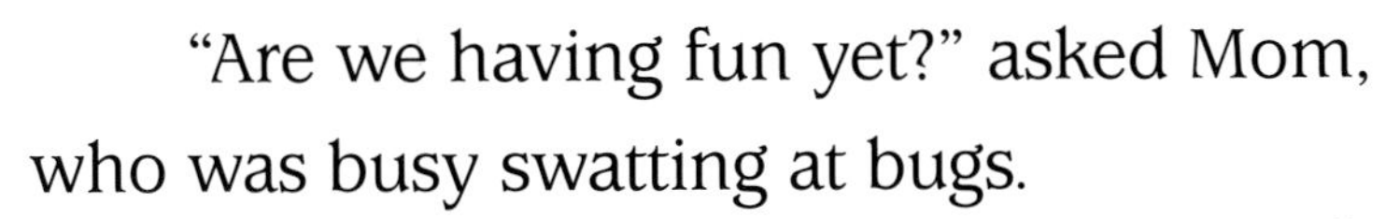

"Are we having fun yet?" asked Mom, who was busy swatting at bugs.

"You'll love bugs once you get to know them," I said.

"Yuk," she said.

"Don't say 'yuk,' say 'wow,'" I told her as I uncovered a shimmery slug. She was getting interested until Simon shouted.

"Hey, Mom, try surfing this web for a change."

Mom took a quick look.

"The female of this species will kill her mate if provoked," Simon said.

Mom smiled at Dad, then looked more closely.

"What a sweet little spider," she said.

My eyes are so amazing I can find those little black dots that mice leave, except I don't say anything 'cause they really gross Dad out.

He wasn't a big fan when Simon found some big dots a raccoon left behind.

"Look closely," Simon explained, "and you can tell what kind of animal left it by the size and the bits of berries or bones or fur ..."

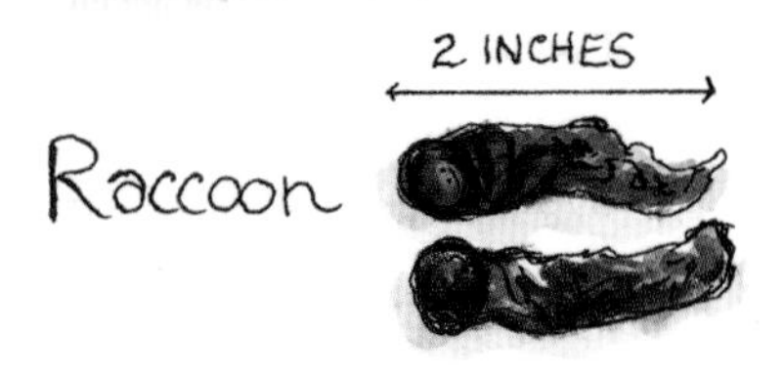

"Enough, Simon!" said Dad. "Let's concentrate on animal tracks."

Simon ran ahead. In the mud it was easy to see chipmunk tracks, raccoon tracks and Simon tracks. Suddenly Simon's tracks disappeared and some really scary tracks appeared!

"I'm afraid something very ferocious indeed has eaten our young son," Dad said. "Let's check the scat for glasses and bits of baseball cap!"

"Very funny, Dad," I said. But I ran ahead as fast as I could just in case.

## Simon's Scary Tracks

YOU'LL NEED:

- an empty aluminum drink can (the pop-top kind) for each foot

Place the drink can on its side. Put your foot in the middle of it (either your heel or the front of your shoe) and press firmly until the edges curl around and attach to your shoe.

Walk on soft earth to make tracks.

I found Simon sitting on a log removing the cans he had used to make his scary steps.

"I don't know about anyone else, but I'm ready to head back," I said.

"So soon," said Mom.

# Fun Lunch Contest

## Tuna Turtles

YOU'LL NEED:
- ✯ 7oz. (184 g) can of tuna fish, drained
- ✯ 1/4 cup (50 mL) mayonnaise
- ✯ 1/3 cup (85 mL) finely chopped celery
- ✯ 2 tbsp. (30 mL) finely chopped red onion (op)

- ✯ 2 large pita bread rounds or 6 mini pitas for baby turtles
- ✯ sweet or dill pickles

Break the tuna into small chunks with a fork and mix in mayonnaise, celery and onion.

Cut an opening about one-quarter of the way into the pita.

Stuff one half of the tuna filling into each large pita.

Place the pita on a plate and turn it into a turtle by adding pickle slices, as shown.

Cut 2 slices of pickle in half and use for turtle feet.

Cut the rounded tip from a pickle. Stick a toothpick into it and fasten it to the pita for your turtle's head.

**Tip:**
Decorate your turtle's shell with slices of olive stuck on with cream cheese "glue".

"Our next exciting event is a fun lunch contest," we announced.

"Great!" said Mom as she squeezed the rain out of her sweatshirt,

"That means that boring old tuna fish sandwiches are out," I said.

"But tuna turtles are in!" Simon whooped.

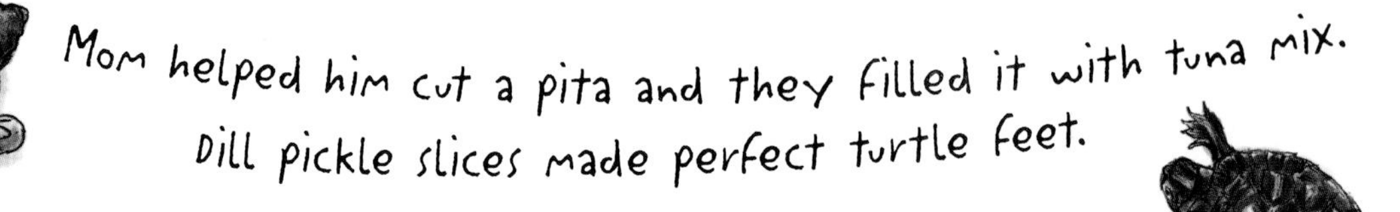

Mom helped him cut a pita and they filled it with tuna mix. Dill pickle slices made perfect turtle feet.

"Mom likes spiders now, so I made one!"



**Tip:**

Use the spread as glue and stick two raisins or chocolate chips on your spider for eyes.

All Dad could come up with was "ants on a log," which he must have made a million years ago in nursery school!



"I'm sailing a celery boat," boasted Mom.

It was easy to see I still had another chance to win. I stuck a straw through a paper cup and turned a marshmallow into a pop-up puppet in about two seconds.

"No offense, everyone," said Simon (who had just named himself the contest judge), but tuna turtles are the most fun so far.

## Can-do Ice Cream

YOU'LL NEED: 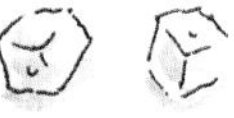

- ✯ 2 clean metal cans with lids. Make sure one can fits in the other with space around it. (Different-sized coffee cans are perfect.)
- ✯ 1 cup (250 mL) half-and-half cream
- ✯ 1/2 cup (125 mL) white sugar
- ✯ 1 tsp. (5 mL) vanilla
- ✯ 2 tbsp. (30 mL) salt
- ✯ ice cubes

In the smaller can mix the cream, sugar, and vanilla. Seal the lid on tightly.

Place it in the larger can. Add enough ice around the can until it is covered. (You may have to smash some of the cubes to fit!)

Sprinkle with salt. Seal the lid on tightly. (If you're worried about a few leaks seal the cans with duct tape and do the rolling on an old sheet.)

Sit on the floor and roll the can back and forth non-stop for 15 minutes.

**Tip:**
On a very warm day, chill cans in the fridge first.

"Well," said Dad, "there was a time when families found it fun to spend an afternoon churning their own ice cream."

"The winner!!!" we shouted. "Let's do it!"

"If only we could," he sighed.

"Maybe we can!" said Mom as she got out an empty coffee can.

"Surely we can't shake that can for the rest of the day!" said Dad.

"Just watch me!" Mom said, rolling the can across the room.

We all joined her.

Fifteen minutes flew by as we rolled the can, chanting, "You scream, I scream, we all scream for ice cream!!" And like magic, it was ready!

We sat slurping the sweet, shivery ice cream, until the sun came out from behind the clouds.

## Solar Sipping Tea

YOU'LL NEED:

- ✩ 1 quart (1 L) glass jar with a lid
- ✩ 2 tea bags
- ✩ slices of orange and/or lemon

Place the sliced fruit in the jar and fill with water.

Add the tea bags.

Screw on the lid and place in full sun for two hours or so.

Taste. When ready take out the tea bags.

Pour over ice. Add sugar or honey and crushed mint leaves.

### Tip:

You may have to move the jar as the shade spreads.

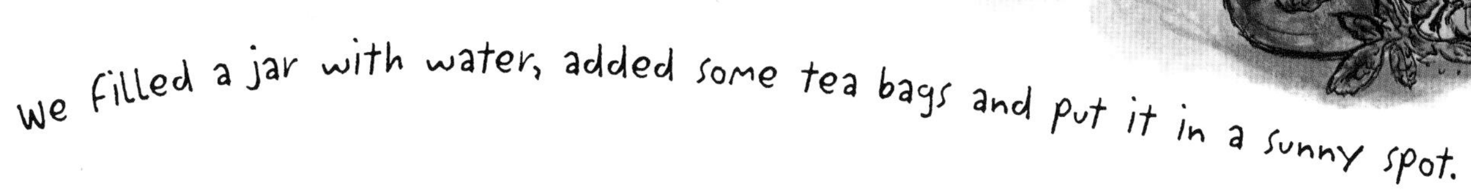


"You'll have to wait for your tea today," I told Mom and Dad. "Mother Nature's making it and she always takes a little longer."

# Trophies of the Trail

## Woven Web Hanging

YOU'LL NEED:

- ☆ paper plate
- ☆ string, yarn, or floss
- ☆ scissors

Cut a triangle design around the edge of the plate. (If you are not very good with scissors see the Tip.)

Cut small slits with the scissors where the triangles join.

Tie a knot in a very long piece of string and insert it into one of the slits.

Wind the string from slit to slit. Make sure you cross the plate's center each time.

When you get to the last slit, make a loop for hanging and tie a knot.

Tuck your treasures (feathers, ferns, strips of bark, flowers, etc.) into the strings.

### Tip:

An easier way is to omit the triangle design and simply cut slits around the edges.

Simon and I were busy sorting through all the neat stuff we got on the hike – a partridge feather, shiny stones, sticky little burrs, papery birch bark, a gazillion acorns, pinecones, a humongous fungus for writing on and some feathery ferns.

The spider's web we saw on the hike gave me an idea.

Then I cut slits and wrapped some string around the plate like a web and stuck in my favorite treasures.

Simon looked up each one of his things in the field guide. He's not happy until everything has a proper name.

I drew faces on my acorns and gave each of mine a name, too, until Simon swiped one and threw it. I threw one and tried to hit his, and before you knew it, we turned it into an awesome tossing game.

## Awesome Toss Game

YOU'LL NEED:

☆ a small pile of acorns

HOW TO PLAY:

The first player tosses an acorn about 10 feet (3 m) away.

The other players, in turn, try to toss their acorn as close to the first one as possible.

The player who gets the closest is the winner and gets to toss the first acorn for the next round.

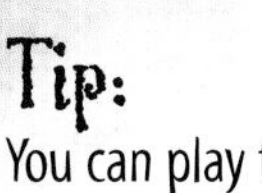

**Tip:**

You can play this game with chestnuts, pinecones, pebbles and shells, too.

## Brave Knight's Sword

YOU'LL NEED:
(for each sword)
- 3 full sheets of newspaper
- 1 single sheet of newspaper
- tape

BLADE
Arrange the 3 sheets of newspaper one on top of the other.
Roll tightly starting at the longer side.
Tape edge closed.
Flatten the roll.
Fold the corners of one end into a point.

HANDLE
Roll up the single sheet of newspaper, starting at the shorter side.
Tape edge closed.
Flatten the roll.
Roll about 3"(7 cm) in from each end. Tape. Place the handle guard about 8" (20 cm) from the end of the blade and tape in place.
Fold the (non-pointed) end of the blade over the handle.
Tape well.

We could hear the red squirrels scolding each other but Mom and Dad were way too quiet. We found them stretched out, doing absolutely nothing.

"See what happens when they're left on their own. Dad has his nose in a newspaper and Mom is just staring at the sky. Our game *must* wait," Simon said. "A lord and lady languish on the dock." (Simon's best on a quest.)

"We can't be brave knights without magic swords," I said. We slipped a section of newspaper from the pile.

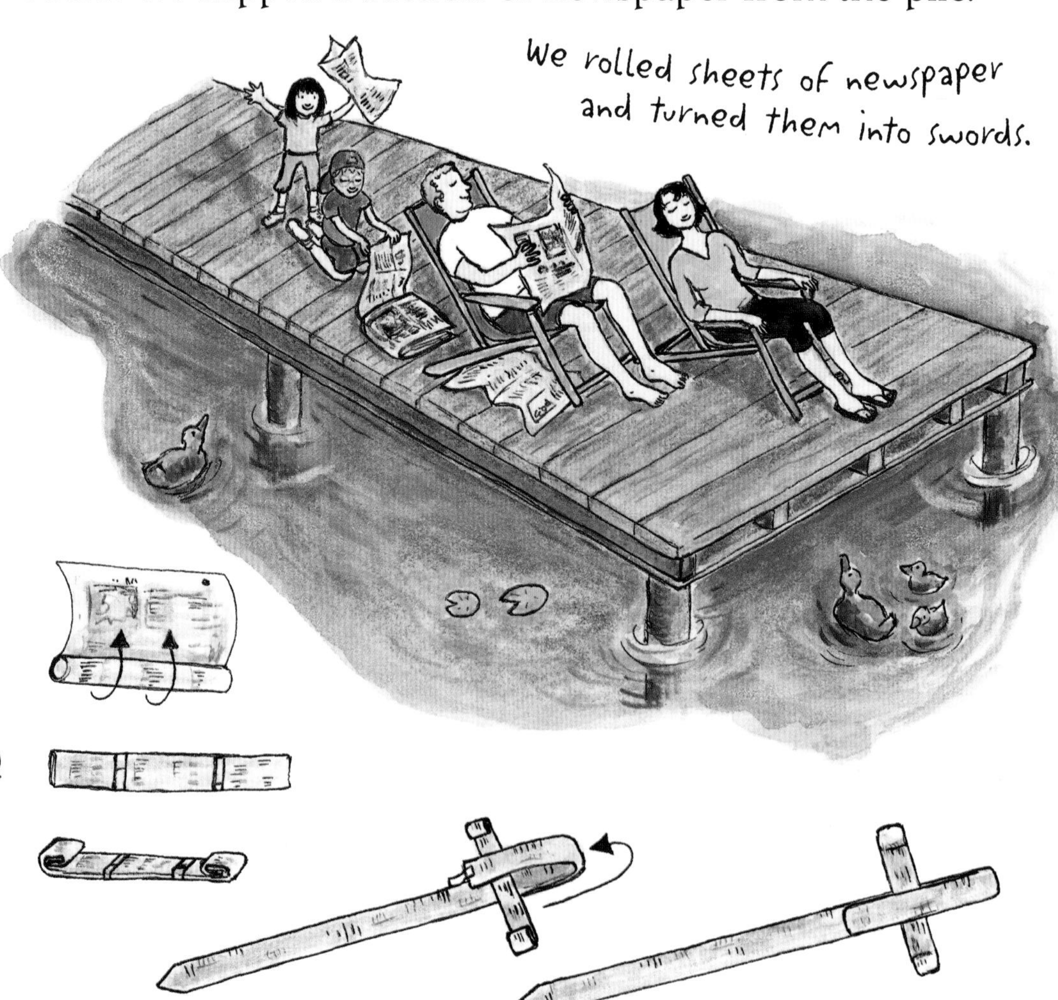


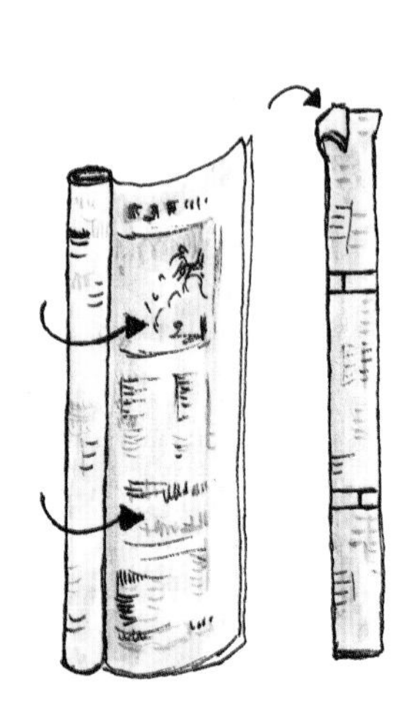

Then we swooped down to the dock, waving our swords, and whisked our parents out of their chairs.

Our parents love whacking balls with rackets and clubs. We showed them how to use paws instead.

We blew up balloons and made our paws by sticking paper plates together.

Soon Mom and Dad were splashing and laughing, so we could slip away.

"I think we're safe for a while," said Simon. "We can plan the rest of our rescue."

## Paddle Paws

YOU'LL NEED:

- 4 paper plates for each player (2 for each hand)
- stapler or glue
- crayons or markers
- balloons

Cut a section (about 1/3) off one of the plates to make a space to slip your hand (just like you did for the weatherperson puppet).

Draw a paw print on the other plate.

Staple or glue plates together.

Make a "paw" for each hand.

Choose teams and swat the balloon back and forth.

When a team can't hit the balloon the opposing team scores a point.

**Tip:**

Try blowing up several balloons. Have everyone try to keep them all in the air at the same time.

# Dad's Bad Attitude

## Folded Butterfly

YOU'LL NEED:

- 2 squares of newspaper (one larger than the other). For example, the larger 10" (25 cm) square and the smaller 8"(20 cm) square.
- paper clip

Accordion-fold each square.
Here's how:

1. Place a paper square in front of you on a table. Starting at a pointed corner, fold a strip that is about 1" (2.5 cm). Don't unfold it.
2. Turn the paper over and fold it again. Make this width the same as the first.
3. Again turn the paper over and make a new fold. Keep doing this until you have folded the whole piece of paper.
4. When you have finished folding each square, pinch it in the middle and hold closed.
5. Place the smaller folded paper on top of the larger and hold together with the paper clip.

### Tip:

To make a cat toy, tie a string on your butterfly.

No sooner were our parents out of the water than they were back in their chairs. Dad was rummaging around for the sports section, which we had to confess was now our two trusty swords. He reached for another.

"Oh, no, that section makes you write mad letters," I said. "I can show you how to use the news to make a butterfly instead!"

"It's actually a moth," said Simon. "Butterflies rest with their wings upright."

"It's too fiddly for me," said Dad.

"How about a nice big bowl for your snacks."

"Now you're talking!" he said. "But I'd better warn you, I was all thumbs in school!"

"Just work with me here, Dad. It's only water and newspaper. Nothing to be afraid of. I know you'll be great at it."

## Dad's Snack Bowl

YOU'LL NEED:
- a round-bottomed bowl
- 8 single (not the full 2-page spread) sheets of newspaper

Turn the bowl upside down on a flat surface.

Wet one sheet of newspaper in a pan of warm water. (Make sure it's completely wet.)

Lay it over the bowl. Smooth with your hands and press down firmly around the edge.

Lay another wet sheet over the bowl in an alternate direction.

Repeat this procedure (remember to alternate each layer) until all the newspaper sheets have been used.

Allow to dry (overnight or for a sunny afternoon).

The newspaper bowl will lift off easily when it is dry.

Trim the edges with scissors.

Decorate with markers or paint.

**Tip:**
For a smaller bowl, use 4 single sheets torn in half.

And he was. It turns out that he actually has eight perfectly good fingers and only two sort of fumble-y thumbs.

We rushed to the dock to work more magic.

# Lakeside Spa

## Mom's Sun Hat

YOU'LL NEED:
- 3 full sheets of newspaper
- masking tape
- scissors

Place the sheets of paper over your mom's head.

Alternate the direction of each sheet as you put it on.

Lightly mold it to her head.

Wrap masking tape around her head two or three times – just above her ears. (You might need an extra pair of hands to hold the newspaper in place while you do this.)

Remove the newspaper hat and trim the brim to the size you want.

Decorate with flowers, ferns or feathers.

"I'm really just enjoying doing nothing," Mom protested.

She was as bored as beans and being brave. The walls and I knew it.

"Don't say another word," I said, and she couldn't because I had just covered her head with the classified section.

"What are you doing?" she managed to mutter, peering out from under the used car ads.

"You're getting too much sun," I told her, "so I'm making you a sun hat."

**Tip:**
You can make a short-brimmed fishing hat by cutting more off.

I wrapped masking tape round and round the newspaper on her head.

Simon trimmed it with scissors so it would have a nice floppy brim.

I used some of my favorite flowers, ferns and feathers to decorate it.

## Monster Mash

YOU'LL NEED:
- ☆ 1/2 ripe avocado
- ☆ 1 tbsp. (15 mL) rolled oats
- ☆ 1 tsp. (5 mL) olive oil

Mash the avocado in a bowl with a fork.

Stir in rolled oats and oil and mix until it makes a smooth paste.

Spread on your face and allow to dry for 1/2 hour.

Rinse with warm water.

"I hope you didn't have any big plans for this avocado," Simon said.

"We found a recipe for an amazing mask in your magazine. It will restore your face to its former natural beauty."

"From your lips to God's ear," said Mom.

We mashed avocado and mixed it with rolled oats and oil and smeared it on our faces.

We looked like green monsters.

"Now for something to relieve your stress," said Simon.

## Squishy Stress Balls

YOU'LL NEED:
(for each stress ball)
- 1 balloon, helium quality
- about 1/3 cup (75 mL) sand (rice, barley, flour also work well)
- funnel (or top cut off a plastic pop bottle)
- permanent marker (op)

Stretch the neck of the balloon over the funnel tip.

Pour the sand into the funnel and work it into the balloon.

Tie a knot in the balloon.

Write the person's name or draw a face with marker.

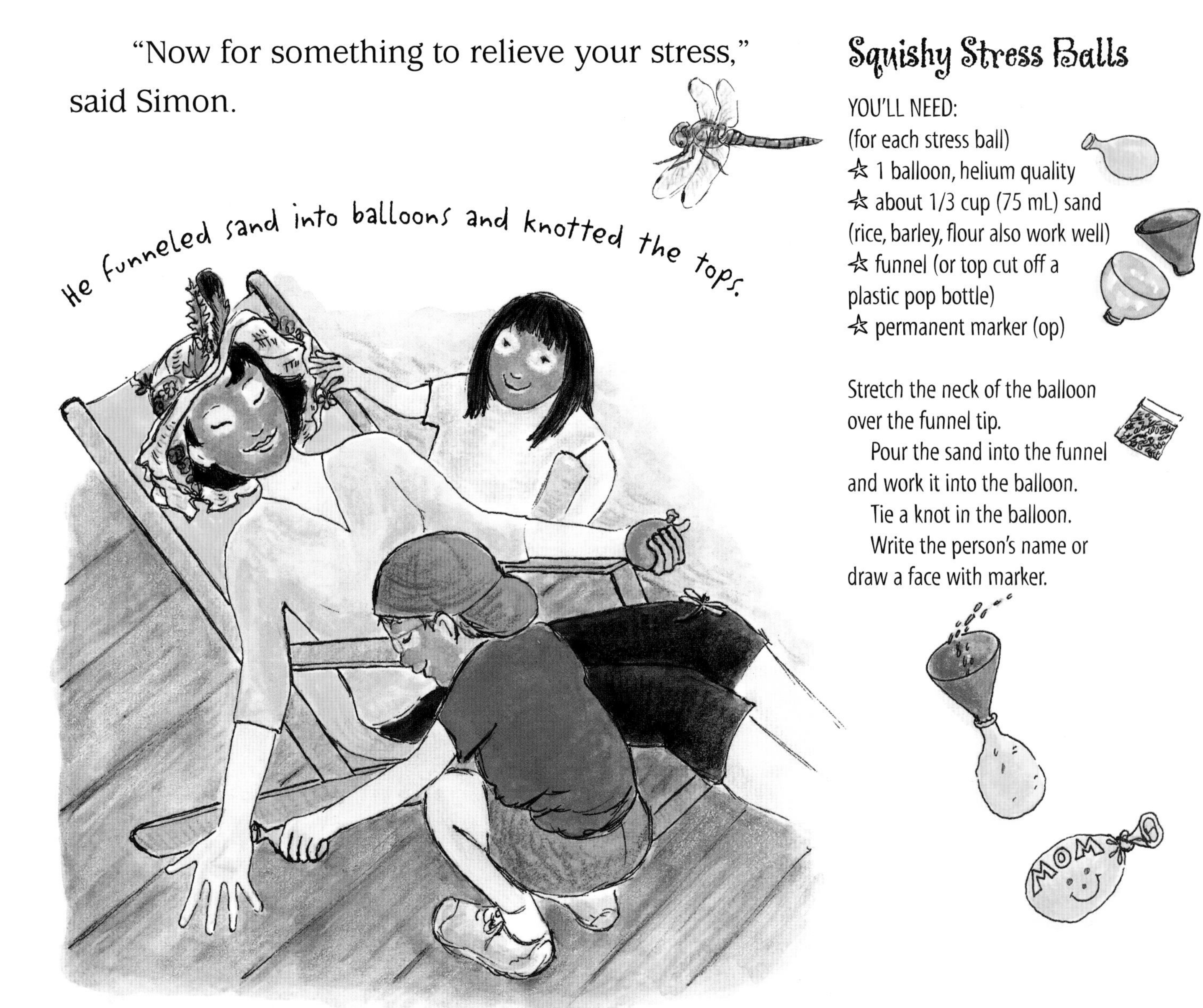


"Squeeze these and your tension will simply melt away," he said and plopped one in each of Mom's hands.

Dad poured the sun tea over ice, while he waited for his bowl to dry.

I told Mom to lie back and sip her tea and I would keep the bugs away.

"Oh, bugs are no bother," she said. "Look, a beautiful dragonfly just landed on my knee."

**Tip:**
To make it easier to fill, stretch the balloon by blowing it up about halfway, then letting the air out.

## Gyotaku

YOU'LL NEED:
- ✯ fresh fish (either caught or from the market)
- ✯ newspaper
- ✯ paint
- ✯ a small stiff paintbrush
- ✯ pins for positioning the fish's fins (op)
- ✯ newsprint or any other absorbent paper, even paper towel

Place the fish on a surface covered with newspaper.

Spread the fins and tail. Hold in place with pins (op).

Brush a thin layer of paint all over the fish.

Place your paper on the fish to cover it completely.

Rub gently over the entire surface to transfer the inked impression of the fish to the paper.

Carefully peel off the paper. Allow to dry.

We were ready for what the magazine called the soothing sport of fishing. We let Mom pick whichever worm she wanted from our wiggling pile.

Mom must have picked the right one 'cause she is the only one who caught a fish.

"How can we make sure Mom never forgets her catch?" I asked.

"Gyotaku," said Simon with the smug look he always gets, "which means fish rubbing, and it originated in Asia as a way of recording the fish that was caught."

We spread some paint on the fish,

then we placed a sheet of paper on it and rubbed gently.

When we peeled the paper off we had an amazing fish.

"What'll we do with the fish now!?"

"Simple," said Simon. "We'll do what the very first people who lived here did.

"We'll bury our fish, and then make a garden with corn, bean and squash seeds. The corn grows and the bean wraps itself around the corn stalk and the squash spreads and keeps the garden weed-free. All made possible by the fertilizing of our friendly little fish."

# Salsa Surprise Supper

## Snake Stew

YOU'LL NEED:

- ☆ 1 lb. (500 g) ground beef (or 1 pkg. 12 oz. (340 g) of soy protein substitute)
- ☆ 1 can 10 oz. (284 mL) condensed tomato soup
- ☆ 1 can 14 oz. (398 mL) baked beans in tomato sauce
- ☆ 1 cup (250 mL) salsa
- ☆ 1/2 cup (125 mL) milk

- ☆ 6–8 medium tortillas
- ☆ 1 cup (250 mL) cheddar cheese (grated)

Brown the ground beef. Drain off grease.

Add soup, beans, milk, salsa, and half the cheese.

Cut the tortillas into strips and stir into mix.

Spoon ingredients into a 9″x13″ (22x33 cm) pan.

Add spiral tortilla on top (op) and sprinkle with the rest of the cheese.

Bake at 400°F (200°C) until hot and bubbly. About 25 minutes.

"We can't have boring burritos for supper," I whispered. "The meat's cooked and there are bowls of salsa and cheese ready. Let's see what happens if we dump everything together!"

Simon found canned soup and beans and stirred them in with the stuff mom left. He added some milk so it would mix up all nice and squishy.

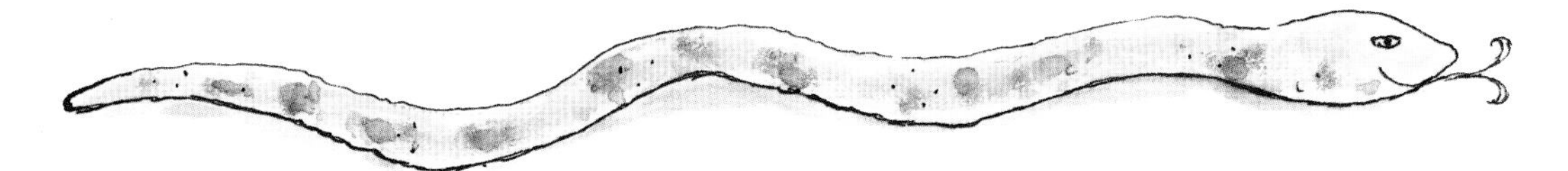

"I'm making snakes from the tortillas to slither through your salsa stew," I said.

"Oh, man," said Simon. "Now what are we supposed to wrap the filling in!"

"Who needs wrapping," I said, as I stirred in my snakes. "I'm covering it all with a swirly tortilla."

It looked so cool you wouldn't believe it.

## Fortune Noodles

YOU'LL NEED:
- ✩ large hollow pasta (for example, cannelloni)
- ✩ marker or nail polish
- ✩ strips of paper with fortunes written on them

Decorate each noodle with a marker or nail polish.

Roll fortunes so they'll fit into the noodle.

Put one at each person's place.

"It appears things are getting pretty fancy indeed," said Dad, wearing his latest creation. "Maybe I'll use my artistic skills to make fortune favors for the table."

We helped Dad write funny family fortunes and decorate the pasta.

HUMMINGBIRDS NEVER REMEMBER THE WORDS TO SONGS

ONLY AN OWL GIVES A HOOT WHAT OTHERS THINK

THE CURE TO BOREDOM IS CURIOSITY

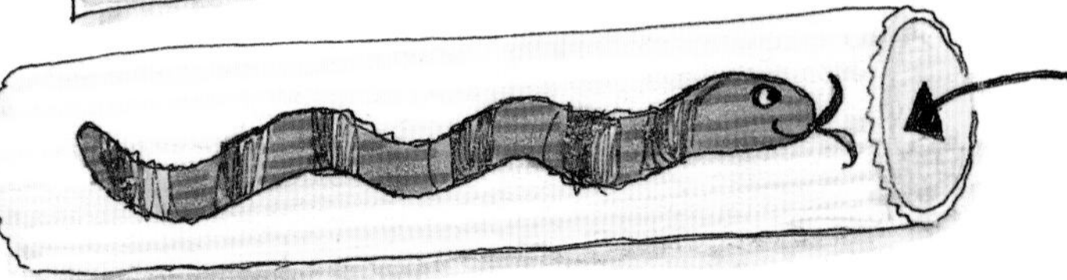

"And for dessert," proclaimed Simon. "Chocolate microwaved mousse!!"

"I don't think a moose can fit in the microwave," I told Yoyo. "He must have meant mouse."

## Moose in a Mug

YOU'LL NEED:
(for each mug)

- 1-1/2 tsp. (7 mL) cornstarch
- 1/2 cup (125 mL) milk
- 1/4 cup (50 mL) semi-sweet chocolate chips
- pinch of salt

Mix milk, cornstarch, and salt together in a mug.

Stir in the chocolate chips.

Microwave on High for one minute.

Stir well.

Microwave on High again for 40 seconds or so until just beginning to boil.

Cool and serve with a spoonful of whipped cream or Can-do ice cream (p.24)!

We each made mousse in our own mug.
Mom held my mug while I stirred.

"I prefer cooking over a campfire," said Dad, as he licked every last bit of his chocolate mousse. "But we'll let it go this time!"

# Fun In A Flash

## Salamander Snap

Deal the whole deck of cards among the players.

Each player straightens his pile and keeps it (face-down) in front of him. No looking at the cards allowed!

The dealer goes first and turns up one card and puts it (face-up) in the center of the table. In turn, each player does the same, making a pile of cards.

Players continue until a player puts a card on top of a card that matches his. For example, a 4 of hearts on a 4 of clubs.

When this happens the first player to notice it and shout "SNAP" (or whatever name you decide) wins.

This player now adds (face-down) the pile of cards in the center of the table to the bottom of the pack in front of him.

A player who calls out "SNAP" at the wrong time must give one of his face-down cards to each of his opponents.

The first player to win all the cards in the deck in this way is the winner of the game.

It was still light after supper so we played cards at the picnic table. We called our game Salamander Snap. Instead of "snap," each of us made an animal sound like "grrrr" or "ribbit" or a loony yodel, until Dad told us to be salamanders and just whisper a soft salamander sound.

We played and played until it was too dark to see the numbers.

We ran and got our flashlights.

## Flashlight in a Jar

YOU'LL NEED:
- jar with a screw-top lid
- inexpensive flashlight
- sturdy string

Put the lighted flashlight into the jar. (Add sand if extra weight is needed.)

Tie the string around the neck of the jar and lower into the lake.

We each put one into a jar and lowered it into the water on a string.

Mom would rather swim in city pools. She doesn't like to swim where she can't see what's on the bottom. Our flashlights shone underwater and showed her all the neat snails and clams and minnows that live there.

"Wow!" she said.

### Switch Story Game

All you'll need for this game is your imagination.

HOW TO PLAY:
Someone starts a story and tells it until another player yells "SWITCH" and takes over telling the story.

Continue playing until each player has a turn.

Soon the only lights we needed were the fireflies and stars and the crackling campfire. Simon made a scary face with his flashlight and started a story.

"Once upon a time there was a humongous, hairy monster that lived in the forest. He was bigger than the trees, bigger than the ..." Simon went on so long that Dad boomed "Switch" and took over.

The monster was very hungry. He snacked on a kayak. He stuffed his mouth with motorboats but he was still hungry. "I'll try a tent full of tasty children next," he growled.

"Yikes!" I said.

"Switch!" said Mom.

She continued the story.

The monster's mom knew that some chewy, gooey canoes would fill up her hungry son, and they did.

## Crunchy Canoe

YOU"LL NEED:
(for each canoe)

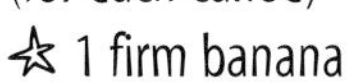

- 1 firm banana
- 1 tbsp. (15 mL) crunchy granola, mini-marshmallows, and/or chocolate chips

Do not peel the banana.

Slice it lengthwise, along the inside curve.

Press the granola, marshmallows, and chocolate chips into the opening.

Wrap with a double thickness of aluminum foil.

Lay it on hot coals for 8–10 minutes until the chocolate and marshmallows melt.

Let the canoe cool slightly, then eat with a spoon from your banana bowl.

**Tip:**
Rainforest Munch (p.18) makes a delicious filling.

We ate them with a spoon 'til it was time for bed.

The baby kingbirds are asleep in their nest above the window but not Simon and me. We have too much to talk about – about how Mom and Dad have learned so much they won't have to worry about being bored ever again, and about how they never even guessed we knew they were worried, and about how we can start making our fort first thing in the morning.

"Maybe we can even make a fort with your friends when we get home, right, Simon?" I said.

He didn't answer. I guess I'd talked him to sleep again.

"Well, good night, Yoyo.
Good night, loons."

"Good night, Lily," said
Mom and Dad through the wall.

Design: Sheryl Shapiro

Annick Press Ltd.


We acknowledge the support of the Canada Council for the Arts, the Ontario Arts Council, and the Government of Canada through the Book Publishing Industry Development Program (BPIDP) for our publishing activities.

**Cataloging in Publication**

Hunter, Dette, 1943-
38 ways to entertain your parents on summer vacation / by Dette Hunter ; art by Kitty Macaulay.

ISBN 1-55037-887-2 (bound).—ISBN 1-55037-886-4 (pbk.)

1. Amusements—Juvenile literature. 2. Handicraft—Juvenile literature. 3. Cookery—Juvenile literature. 4. Parent and child—Juvenile literature.

I. Macaulay, Kitty II. Title. III. Title: Thirty-eight ways to entertain your parents on summer vacation.

TT160.H862 2005 j790.1'91 C2004-906469-X

The art in this book was rendered in watercolor.

Distributed in Canada by:
Firefly Books Ltd.
66 Leek Crescent
Richmond Hill, ON
L4B 1H1

Published in the U.S.A. by Annick Press (U.S.) Ltd.
Distributed in the U.S.A. by:
Firefly Books (U.S.) Inc.
P.O. Box 1338
Ellicott Station
Buffalo, NY 14205

Printed in China.

**Visit us at: www.annickpress.com**



**Acknowledgments**
With thanks to my Aunts Tib and Claire, my sisters and cousins who made summers special, and, of course, Sheryl Shapiro and Annick Press.

*—Dette Hunter*